Spotter's Guide to
BIRDS

Peter Holden
National Organizer of th...

Illustrated by Tre...

Contents

Designed by
Sally Burrough

Edited by
Sue Jacquemier and Sue Tarsky

Printed in Great Britain

First published in 1978 by Usborne Publishing
Limited, 20 Garrick Street, London WC2

Reprinted 1985

Text and Artwork © 1978 by
Usborne Publishing Limited

How to Use this Book

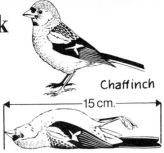

Chaffinch

This book will help you to identify many of the birds you will see in Britain and Europe. Take it with you when you go out spotting. The pictures show the birds perching or flying, depending on how the bird is most often spotted.

There are separate pictures of the females (♀ means female) if they are very different from the males (♂ means male). Sometimes the young, or juvenile, birds are shown too. If a bird's summer and winter plumage (feathers) are very different, both kinds of plumage are shown.

The description next to each bird tells you where to look for it and its size. A bird is measured from the tip of its beak to the tip of its tail (see

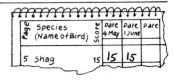

diagram). Birds on the same page are not always drawn to scale.

Each time you spot a bird, make a tick in the small circle next to that bird's picture.

There is a list of special words and their meanings on page 57.

Scorecard

There is a scorecard at the end of the book which gives a score for each bird you spot. A very common bird scores 5 points and a very rare one is 25 points. You can add up your scores after a day out spotting. Because some of the birds are rare in Britain, you can tick

Page	Species (Name of Bird)	Score	Date 4 May	Date 1 June	Date
5	Shag	15	15	15	

off rare birds if you spot them on television or in a film.

Areas Covered by this Book

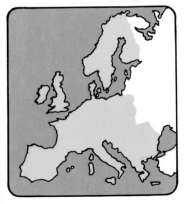

The yellow area on this map shows the countries of Europe where this book can be used to spot birds. Not every bird from each country is in the book, and some birds are not found everywhere in the yellow area. The descriptions in the book always refer to Britain, unless another area is named. Britain, in this book, includes Eire. For example, the description of the Dunlin tells you that it nests on moorland in the north. This means the north of Britain. If a bird is rare in Britain, the description tells you so. Look out for it if you go abroad.

Why Watch Birds?

Birds are everywhere, which makes watching them a good hobby. When you can name the birds you see most often, you may want to know other things about them. There is a list of books to read and clubs to join at the end of the book.

Where to Watch Birds

Start birdwatching in your own garden, or from a window in your home. If there are only a few birds, try putting out food and water to attract more. (See pages 54-55 for instructions on how to make a bird table.) When you can identify all the birds that come to your garden, look in a local park.

Watch ponds or rivers, especially early in the morning before many people are about. School playing fields, old gravel pits and even rubbish tips attract birds. If you go on holiday, you will be able to visit new habitats (places where birds live) and see new species.

Helpful Things to Look for

Notice a bird's shape when it is flying – this will help you identify it. See if it flies in a straight line, glides, bounces or hovers. Note the colour of its plumage and any special markings. What shape is its beak? What colour are its legs and what shape are its feet?

Although bird song is important for identifying birds, it is difficult to describe, and so it is not mentioned much in this book. When you are out spotting, remember to keep your ears, as well as your eyes, open.

Binoculars

As you do more birdwatching, you will probably want to use binoculars. Visit a good shop to try out several pairs. The best sizes are 8x30 or 8x40 (never more than 10x50).

Notebook

Keep a notebook for recording the different birds you see. Write down where and when you see them. Describe any birds you have never seen before. Make quick sketches to help you to identify them later.

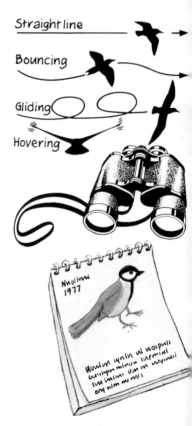

Straight line

Bouncing

Gliding

Hovering

Nuolinw 1977

Shag, Gannet, Cormorant

◄ Shag
Seen all year round. Nests in colonies on rocky coasts. Crest only in nesting season. Like Cormorant, dives for fish. Young are brown. 78 cm.

Shags and Cormorants fly low, close to the water

◄ Gannet
Look out to sea close to the waves for Gannets. Plunges head first into the sea to catch fish. Young are darker. 92 cm.

Cormorant ▼
Usually seen near the sea but sometimes inland in winter. Some have grey head and neck in the breeding season. Nests in colonies on rocky ledges. 92 cm.

White patch in breeding season

Geese

Brent Goose ▶
Look for this small, dark goose on estuaries in winter. 58 cm.

Canada Goose ▶
A large, noisy goose. Look in parks. Nests in the wild in Britain. 95 cm.

Brent Goose

Canada Goose (this bird was introduced from Canada)

Greylag Goose ▼
Nests wild in Scotland and some breed further south. Wild birds from Europe can be seen near coasts in winter. 82 cm.

More white on head than Canada Goose

◀ Barnacle Goose
Look on the west coasts of Britain and Ireland in winter. Sometimes in parks. 63 cm.

Geese, Swans

Pink-footed Goose

◀ Pink-footed Goose

A winter visitor. Seen in large numbers on some fields of young wheat or stubble. 68 cm.

◀ Bean Goose

A rare winter visitor from northern Europe. Grazes on inland pastures or fields of young corn. 80 cm.

Bean Goose

White-fronted Goose ▶

A winter visitor, liking marshes, estuaries and farmland. Look for white at base of bill. 71 cm.

Bewick's Swan

Whooper Swan

Mute Swan

◀ Swans

The Mute is Britain's most common swan, often seen in town parks or on wide rivers. The other two come to Britain in winter and can be seen on lakes, flooded fields or even the sea. Their long necks help them feed in deep water. Whooper 152cm, Bewick's 122 cm, Mute 152 cm.

Ducks

Mallard Teal Wigeon

Duck

Drake

◀ Mallard
Found near most inland waters. Only the female, or duck, gives the familiar "quack". 58 cm.

Duck

Drake

Teal ▶
Smallest European duck. A very shy bird. It prefers the shallow edges of lakes. Flies with fast wing beats. 35 cm.

Duck

Drake

◀ Wigeon
Sometimes seen grazing on fields near water. Forms flocks in winter especially near the sea. Male's call is a loud "wheeo". 46 cm.

Pintail ▶
Uses its long neck to feed on plants under the water. Look for these birds in winter near the sea. 66 cm.

Duck

Drake

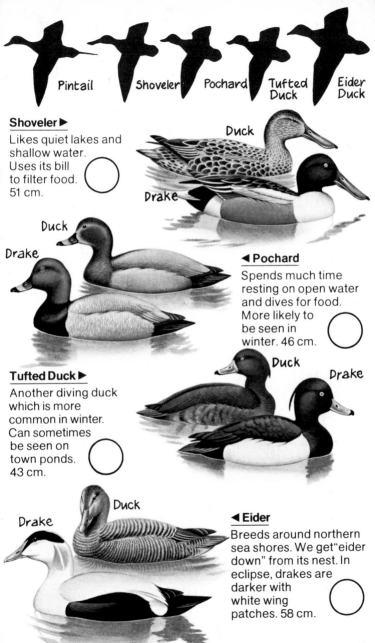

Pintail Shoveler Pochard Tufted Duck Eider Duck

Shoveler ▶
Likes quiet lakes and shallow water. Uses its bill to filter food. 51 cm.

Duck

Drake

Duck

Drake

◀ Pochard
Spends much time resting on open water and dives for food. More likely to be seen in winter. 46 cm.

Tufted Duck ▶
Another diving duck which is more common in winter. Can sometimes be seen on town ponds. 43 cm.

Duck

Drake

Duck

Drake

◀ Eider
Breeds around northern sea shores. We get "eider down" from its nest. In eclipse, drakes are darker with white wing patches. 58 cm.

9

Ducks

Goldeneye ▶

A few nest in Scotland, but mainly a winter visitor. Seen on the sea and inland lakes. Often in flocks. Dives frequently. 46 cm.

Duck

Drake

White wing patches in flight

Short crest ➤

Duck

Drake

◀ Red-breasted Merganser

Breeds by lakes and rivers, often seen near the sea. Seldom seen inland in winter, but visits many coastal areas. Dives for fish. 58 cm.

Goosander ▶

Most British Goosanders nest in Scotland. Likes large lakes in winter. Dives for fish. Look for the shaggy crest on the female. 66 cm.

White throat ➤

Duck

Drake

Female has no knob on bill

Drake

◀ Shelduck

Common around most coasts, especially sheltered estuaries. Often in flocks. Flies slowly with neck stretched out. Looks heavy in flight. 61 cm.

Grebes, Heron, Stork

Great Crested Grebe ▶

Found on inland waters.
Dives for fish. Seldom flies.
Beautiful courtship
displays in spring.
Sometimes seen
on sea in winter.
48 cm.

Crest expands
during display

Winter

Summer

◀ Little Grebe or Dabchick

Common on inland waters,
but secretive and
hard to spot. Call is
a shrill trill. 27 cm.

Winter

Summer

Grey Heron ▶

Usually seen near water.
Nests in colonies in trees.
Eats fish, frogs, small
mammals. Stands
still for long
periods. 92 cm.

Head is drawn
back and legs
stick out
when flying

◀ White Stork

Very rare in Britain. Likes
wet areas. Will nest on
buildings
in Europe.
102 cm.

Birds of Prey

Osprey ▶

Rare summer visitor to Britain. Some nest in Scotland. Plunges into water to catch fish. Often perches on dead trees. 56 cm.

Upper parts a dark brown

◀ Golden Eagle

Lives in Scottish Highlands. Young birds have white on wings and tail. Glides for long distances. Bigger than Buzzard. 83 cm.

Long broad wings

Wings narrower than Buzzard's

Red Kite ▶

This rare bird nests in oak woods in mid-Wales. Soars for long periods. Rare. 62 cm.

Long forked tail

Birds of Prey

Notice the pale wing patches

◄ Buzzard
A large bird of prey with broad rounded wings. Often seen soaring over-moors and farmland as it hunts. Rare in south and eastern England. 54 cm.

♀

Female is larger and browner than male

Sparrowhawk ►
Broad-winged hawk. Hunts small birds along hedges and woodland edges. Never hovers. Female 38 cm. Male 30 cm.

♂

Long pointed wings and long tail

♀

◄ Kestrel
Well-known for the way it hovers when hunting, especially alongside motorways. Some nest in towns. Eats birds, mammals, insects. 34 cm.

♂

Birds of Prey

Tail shorter and wings longer than Kestrel

◀ Hobby

Catches flying insects and birds in the air. Summer visitor to southern England. Look on heaths and downs.
33 cm.

Peregrine ▶

Sea cliffs or inland crags. Hunts over estuaries and marshes in winter. Dives on flying birds at great speed.
38–48 cm.

◀ Goshawk

Looks like a large Sparrowhawk. Lives in dense woods. Rare in Britain. Male 48 cm. Female 58 cm.

Honey Buzzard ▶

Summer visitor to British woodlands. Eats mainly grubs of wasps and bees.
51-59 cm.

Rails, Crake

◄ Moorhen

Water bird that lives near ponds, lakes or streams. Unafraid of people in parks, but secretive elsewhere. Juveniles are brown. 33 cm.

Coot ►

Dives a lot. Prefers large lakes. Look for white bill and forehead. Young are grey with pale throats and breasts. Flocks in winter. 38 cm.

◄ Corncrake

Difficult to see as it lives in long grass. Repeats "crex-crex" cry monotonously, especially after dark. Rare in Britain. 27 cm.

Water Rail ►

Secretive bird that lives in reed beds. Listen for its piglet-like squeal. Legs trail in flight. Swims for short distances. 28 cm.

Game Birds

Red Grouse ▶
Willow Grouse ▶

Red Grouse live in
Britain and Ireland,
and Willow Grouse
in northern Europe.
Willow Grouse
is white in
winter.
36 cm.

summer

Willow
Grouse
winter

Red
Grouse

In summer, the
male's plumage is
more brown and
the female's more
yellow than in
autumn

Winter

◀ Ptarmigan

Lives on barren mountain
tops in the north. Has
three different plumages
and is very well
camouflaged.
Allows people to
get close. 34 cm.

Autumn

♀ Female's tail
is forked

♂

Black Grouse ▶

Often found on edge of
moorland, sometimes in
trees, perched or eating
buds. Groups of males
display together
at a lek. Female
41 cm. Male 53 cm.

Male
tail
curv
outwar

Capercaillie ▶

This large bird lives in
coniferous forests in parts
of Scotland. Eats pine
shoots at tips of
branches.
Male 86 cm.
Female 61 cm.

♂

♀

◀ Partridge

Often in small groups. Likes
farmland with hedges. Its call
is a grating "kirr-ic".
Rarer in Ireland.
30 cm.

Pheasant ▶

Lives on farmland with
hedges. Often reared and
shot as game. Roosts in
trees. Nests on ground.
Look for the long
tail. Male 87 cm.
Female 58 cm.

♂ Cock
Pheasants
can vary in
colour and
often have
a white
neck ring

♀

◀ Red-legged Partridge

Common in southern and
eastern Britain. Fields and
open sandy areas.
Often runs rather
than flies. 34 cm.

Waders

White collar in winter

Summer

White wing bars show in flight

◄ Oystercatcher
Usually seen near the sea especially in winter. Often nests inland in Scotland.
43 cm.

Broad, rounded wings

Lapwing ►
A farmland bird which flocks in winter. Looks black and white at a distance. Displays in the air in breeding season. Calls "pee-wit". 30 cm.

Summer

◄ Turnstone
Likes shingle or rocky shores. Turns stones over to find food. Does not nest in Britain, but can be seen here most months. 23 cm.

Winter

When feeding, Plovers run, then pause before running on again. They bend to pick up food in one quick movement.

Waders

Summer

Broad white bar on wing

Ringed Plover ▶

Usually found near the sea, but sometimes by gravel pits inland. Likes sandy or shingle shores. Seen all the year round. 19 cm.

Juvenile

Summer

Wing bar rarely shows in flight

◀ Little Ringed Plover

Summer visitor. Most common in south-east England. Likes gravel pits and shingle banks inland. Legs are yellowish. 15 cm.

Northern Europe

Winter

Southern Europe

Golden Plover ▶

Breeds on upland moors, but found in flocks on lowlands in winter. Legs are blue-grey. 28cm.

Waders

Redshank ▶

Common on sea shores or wet meadows inland. Look for white on rump and rear edges of wings in flight.
28 cm.

Red legs

◀ Greenshank

Rarer and slightly bigger than Redshank. Seen in spring and autumn on coasts or inland. Some nest in northern Scotland.
30 cm.

Common Sandpiper ▶

Common summer visitor to upland streams and lakes. In wet areas on lower land in spring and autumn. Wags tail and bobs often.
20 cm.

Winter

Summer

White wing bar

Summer

◀ Black-tailed Godwit

A few nest in Britain, but more seen on coasts during winter migration.
41 cm.

Waders

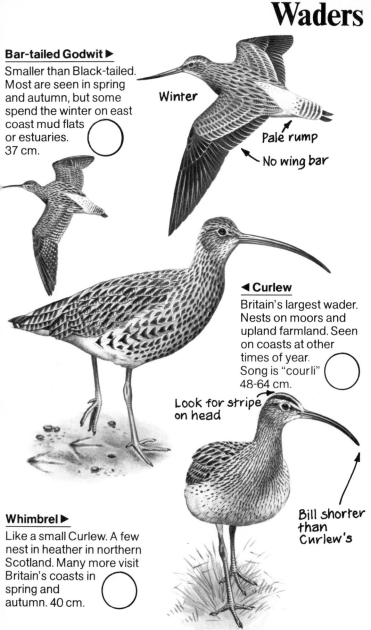

Bar-tailed Godwit ▶
Smaller than Black-tailed. Most are seen in spring and autumn, but some spend the winter on east coast mud flats or estuaries. 37 cm.

Winter

Pale rump

No wing bar

◀ Curlew
Britain's largest wader. Nests on moors and upland farmland. Seen on coasts at other times of year. Song is "courli" 48-64 cm.

Look for stripe on head

Bill shorter than Curlew's

Whimbrel ▶
Like a small Curlew. A few nest in heather in northern Scotland. Many more visit Britain's coasts in spring and autumn. 40 cm.

Waders

◄ Dunlin
A common visitor to sea shores, but nests on moorland in the north. Usually seen in flocks. Beak straight or down-curved. 19 cm.

Winter

Summer

Knot ►
Seen in huge flocks in winter. Likes sand or mud flats in estuaries. Rare inland. Mainly a winter visitor. Breeds in the Arctic. 25 cm.

Winter

◄ Sanderling
Runs back and forth along water's edge on sandy beaches where it catches small animals. Coasts in winter. 20 cm.

Winter

♂ Summer

Ruff ►
Seen in spring and autumn in Britain, but some also winter in wet places. Female 23 cm. Male 29 cm.

♀

Winter ♂

Waders

Woodcock ▶
Secretive bird of damp woods. Watch out for its display flight over woods at dusk in early summer.
34 cm.

Woodcock

◀ Snipe
Lives on wet fields, marshes or lake edges. Hard to see on the ground, but rises up with a zig-zag flight when disturbed.
27 cm.

Avocet ▶
A few nest on coastal marshes in eastern England. Some winter on southern estuaries. Rare inland. 43 cm.

Pigeons, Doves

Woodpigeon ▶
A common bird of farmland, woods and towns. Forms large flocks in winter. 41 cm.

White on wings

Grey rump. No white on wings

Rock Dove ▶
Town pigeons are descended from these birds. Usually found in small groups on sea cliffs. 33 cm.

◀ Stock Dove
Nests in holes in trees or on rock faces. Seen feeding on the ground, often with Woodpigeons. Sometimes seen in flocks. 33 cm.

Town Pigeons

White rump

◀ Collared Dove
Often found in large gardens, parks or around farm buildings. Feeds mainly on grain. Sometimes seen in flocks. 30 cm.

White on tail

Turtle Dove ▶
Summer visitor to England and Wales. Lives in open woods, parks and farmland. Listen for its purring call. 28 cm.

White margin on tail

Auks, Fulmar

Neck and throat are white in winter

Summer

◀ Razorbill
Look for its flat-sided bill. Nests on cliffs and rocky shores in colonies. Winters at sea. Dives for fish. Often with Guillemots. 41 cm.

Neck and throat are white in winter

Guillemot ▶
Nests on cliff ledges in large, noisy groups. Slimmer than Razorbill. Northern birds have a white eye-ring and white line on their heads. 42 cm.

Summer

◀ Fulmar
Nests in colonies on ledges on sea cliffs. Often glides close to waves on stiff wings. Can be seen near cliffs all round our coasts. 47 cm.

Puffin ▶
Rocky islands and sea cliffs in the north and west. Nests between rocks or in burrows in the ground. 30 cm.

Colourful beak and reddish feet in summer

Gulls

Black-headed Gull ▶

Common inland and near the sea. Nests in colonies. Look out for the white front edge of the long wings. Dark brown head in summer only. 37 cm.

Winter

Summer

◀ Lesser Black-backed

Mainly a summer visitor. Seen on the coast or inland, but some winter in Britain. Head is streaked with grey in winter. 53 cm.

Legs are yellow in summer

Great Black-backed Gull ▶

Britain's largest Gull. Not very common inland. Nests on rocky coasts. Often solitary. Legs pinkish. 66 cm.

◀ Common Gull

Some nest in Scotland and Ireland. Seen further south and often inland in winter. 41 cm.

26

Gull, Terns

Summer

◄ Herring Gull

Common on the coast in ports and seaside towns. Scrounges food from people and even nests on buildings. Young's plumage is mottled brown for first three years. 56 cm.

Arctic Tern in summer

Common Tern's bill has black tip

Arctic Tern ►
Common Tern ►

Both species most likely to be seen near sea, but Common Tern also nests inland. Both dive into sea to catch fish. 34 cm.

Summer

Summer

◄ Black Tern

A spring and autumn visitor to Britain. Can be seen flying low over lakes, dipping down to pick food from the surface. 24 cm.

Winter

Summer

Little Tern ►

A summer visitor to Britain which nests in small groups on shingle beaches. Dives for fish. 24 cm.

Look for yellow bill with black tip

27

Owls

Barn Owl ▶

Its call is an eerie shriek. Often nests in old buildings or hollow trees. Hunts small mammals and roosting birds. 34 cm.

Birds with dark faces and breasts are found in north and east Europ

◀ Little Owl

Small, flat-headed ow Flies low over farmlan and hunts at dusk. Nes in tree-holes. Bobs up and down when curious. 22 cm.

Bouncing flight

Tawny Owl ▶

Calls with familiar "hoot". Hunts at night where there are woods or old trees. Eats small mammals or birds. 38 cm.

◀ Pygmy Owl

Smallest European owl. Found in mountain forests, but not in Britain. Has a whistling "keeoo" call. Hunts small birds in flight. 16 cm.

Short-eared Owl ▶

Hunts in daylight and at dusk. Likes open country where it catches voles and other small mammals. Perches on the ground. Fierce-looking. 37 cm.

◀ Long-eared Owl

A secretive night-hunting owl of dense conifer woods. Roosts during the day. Long "ear" tufts cannot be seen in flight. 34 cm.

Tengmalm's Owl ▶

Small owl that lives in forests in northern and central Europe. Very rare visitor to Britain. Hunts at night. Nests in tree-holes. 25 cm.

◀ Scops Owl

Rare visitor to Britain from southern Europe. Gives its monotonous "kiu" call from a hidden perch. Hunts only at night. 19 cm.

Hoopoe, Nightjar, Cuckoo, Kingfisher

Hoopoe ▶

Rare visitor to Britain, seen mainly in spring. More common in southern Europe. Probes ground for insects with long bill. 28 cm.

Nightjar

Male has white spots

◀ Nightjar

Rarely seen in daylight. Listen for its continuous churring after dark when it hunts insects. Summer migrant. Lives on heathland. 27 cm.

Cuckoo ▶

Male's song is well known. Female has bubbling call. Looks like Sparrowhawk in flight. All over Britain in summer. 30 cm.

Usually flies low and straight over water

Juvenile Cuckoo

◀ Kingfisher

Brilliantly coloured. Found near lakes and rivers where it dives for fish. Listen for its shrill whistle. 17 cm.

Woodpeckers

▼ Great Spotted Woodpecker

Size of a Song Thrush. In woods all over Britain. Drums on trees in spring. 23 cm.

Male has red crown

Female has red patch on back of head

Large white patches on wings

♂

▲ Black Woodpecker

Size of a Rook. In forests in Europe, especially old pine woods. Not in Britain. Can be confused with Crow in flight. 46 cm.

▼ Green Woodpecker

Size of a Town Pigeon. Often feeds on ground. Open woods and parks. Quite common in England and Wales. Rare in Scotland. Laugh-like call. 32 cm.

Striped back

♂

Yellow-green rump

▲ Lesser Spotted Woodpecker

Sparrow-sized. Lacks white wing patches of Great Spotted. Male has red crown. Found in open woods. Not in Scotland. 14 cm.

Woodpeckers do not live in Ireland. They all have bouncing flight

31

Swift, Swallow, Martins

Swift ▶

A common migrant that visits Britain from May to August. Flies fast over towns and country in flocks. Listen for its screaming call. 17 cm.

Swift's tail is forked

Swallow's tail has streamers when adult

White underparts

◀ Swallow

Summer migrant seen from April to October. Prefers country, usually near water. Nests on rafters or ledges in buildings. 19 cm.

House Martin ▶

Summer migrant to Britain. Builds a cup-shaped nest under eaves. Is found in town and country. Like the Swallow, it catches insects in flight. 13 cm.

White rum

White underparts

Brown back

Brown band on breast

◀ Sand Martin

Summer migrant. Groups nest in holes in sandy cliffs and other soft banks. Often seen in flocks, catching insects over water. 12 cm.

Larks, Pipits, Dunnock

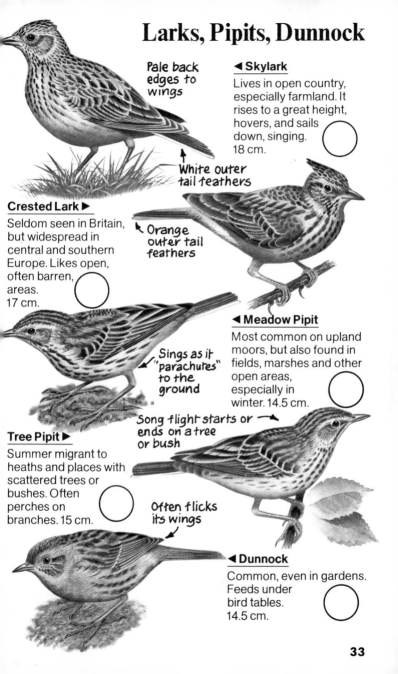

Pale back edges to wings

◄ Skylark
Lives in open country, especially farmland. It rises to a great height, hovers, and sails down, singing. 18 cm.

White outer tail feathers

Crested Lark ►
Seldom seen in Britain, but widespread in central and southern Europe. Likes open, often barren, areas. 17 cm.

Orange outer tail feathers

◄ Meadow Pipit
Most common on upland moors, but also found in fields, marshes and other open areas, especially in winter. 14.5 cm.

Sings as it "parachutes" to the ground

Song flight starts or ends on a tree or bush

Tree Pipit ►
Summer migrant to heaths and places with scattered trees or bushes. Often perches on branches. 15 cm.

Often flicks its wings

◄ Dunnock
Common, even in gardens. Feeds under bird tables. 14.5 cm.

Wagtails

Pied Wagtail ▶
White Wagtail ▶

White Wagtail is widespread in Europe, but in Britain we usually only see the Pied. Common, even in towns. 18 cm.

Pied Wagtail

Juveniles are grey

White Wagtail

All the birds on this page wag their tails up and down.

◀ Grey Wagtail

Usually nests near fast-flowing water in hilly areas. Paler yellow in winter, when it visits lowland waters. Male has black throat. 18 cm.

♂ Summer

Blue-headed Wagtail Central Europe ♂

Yellow Wagtail Britain and Ireland

Ashy-headed Wagtail Southern Europe ♂

Yellow Wagtail ▶
Blue-headed Wagtail ▲

Summer visitor which likes grassy places near water. In Britain we usually see only the Yellow Wagtail. 17 cm.

♂ Spanish Wagtail Spain and Portugal

Females are duller coloured

Waxwing, Dipper, Wren, Shrikes

Resembles a Starling in flight

◄ Waxwing
Rare winter visitor from northern Europe. Feeds on berries and will visit gardens. 17 cm.

Dipper ►
Likes fast-flowing rivers and streams in hilly areas. Bobs up and down on rocks in water. Submerges to find food. 18 cm.

Northern Europe

Britain and Central Europe

Flies fast and straight on tiny, rounded wings

◄ Wren
Found almost everywhere. Loud song finishes with a a trill. Never keeps still for long. 9.5 cm.

Red-backed Shrike ►
Rare summer migrant to heaths in south-east England. Catches and eats insects, small birds, etc. 17 cm.

Stores food by sticking it on thorns

♂ ♀

◄ Great Grey Shrike
Winter visitor to open country where it feeds on birds, mammals. etc. Flies low and often hovers. 24 cm.

Warblers

Sedge Warbler ▶

Summer migrant. Nests in thick vegetation, usually near water, but sometimes in drier areas. Sings from cover and is often difficult to see. 13 cm.

White stripe over eye

Rump is reddish-brown

◀ Reed Warbler

Summer visitor. Nests in reed beds or among waterside plants, mainly in the south of England. Hard to spot. Look for it flitting over reeds. 13 cm.

Brown above, paler below

Garden Warbler ▶

Summer visitor. Sings from dense cover, and is hard to see. Likes woods with undergrowth or thick hedges. Song can be confused with Blackcap's. 14 cm.

♂

Female's cap is reddish-brown

◀ Blackcap

Common summer visitor to woods or places with trees. Always moving from perch to perch as it sings. 14 cm.

♀

Female and young have brown heads

Flight is short and jerky

♂

◄ Whitethroat

A summer migrant, which hides itself in thick, low bushes. Sometimes sings its fast, scratchy song in flight. Flight is short and jerky. 14 cm.

Willow Warbler ►

Summer migrant. Commonest British warbler. Its song, which comes down the scale, is the best way of telling it from the Chiffchaff. 11 cm.

Light – coloured legs

Juvenile is more yellow

◄ Chiffchaff

Summer migrant, often arriving in March. A few spend the winter here. The repetitive "chiff-chaff" song can be heard in woods and from bushes. 11 cm.

Dark legs

Wood Warbler ►

Summer migrant to open woods. Sings from a branch repeating a note faster and faster until it becomes a trill. 13 cm.

Yellow breast, white underparts

Flycatchers, Chats

◄ Pied Flycatcher

Flies after insects and catches them in the air. Also feeds on the ground. Summer migrant to some deciduous woods. 13 cm.

♂

♀

Whinchat ►

Summer migrant. Found in open country. "Tic-tic" call. Perches on tops of bushes and posts. 13 cm.

♀

♂

Flicks wings and tail

◄ Stonechat

Its "tak-tak" call sounds like stones being knocked together. Found on heaths with gorse, especially near the sea. 13 cm.

♀

♂

Colour is duller in winter

Wheatear ►

Summer migrant to moors and barren areas, but also seen elsewhere in spring and in autumn. 15 cm.

♂

♀

White rump and black tail

Flycatchers, Chats

Spotted Flycatcher ▶

Summer migrant. Catches insects in flight. Likes open woods, parks and gardens. 14 cm.

Sits upright, often on a bare branch

♀

◀ Redstart

Summer migrant to open woods, parks and heaths. Constantly flickers its tail. 14 cm.

♀

♂

Black Redstart ▶

A few nest on buildings or on cliffs in Britain. Some winter in the south of England. Flickers its tail. 14 cm.

◀ Robin

A woodland bird that is familiar in gardens. It sings during winter and spring. "Tic-tic" is its call of alarm. Male and female look alike. 14 cm.

Nightingale ▶

Secretive summer migrant. Best found by listening for its song during May and June. 17 cm.

Reddish tail

39

Thrushes, Oriole

Fieldfare ▶

Winter visitor, but a few nest in England and Scotland. Flocks can be seen in autumn, eating berries in hedgerows.
25.5 cm.

◀ Ring Ouzel

Summer migrant to moors and mountains. Visits lower regions on migration. Shyer than Blackbird. Listen for loud piping call. 24 cm.

♂
♀

♀
♂

Young are lighter and spottier than female

Blackbird ▶

Lives where there are trees and bushes, often in parks and gardens. Some Blackbirds are part albino and have some white feathers.
25 cm.

♂
♀

◀ Golden Oriole

Rare summer migrant most likely to be seen in thick woods of England or Wales. Difficult to see as it spends a lot of time in tree-tops. 24 cm.

Thrushes, Starling

White stripe over eye →

◀ Redwing

Winter migrant, but a few nest in Scotland. Seen feeding on berries in hedges or hunting worms on grass. 21 cm.

Song Thrush ▶

Found near or in trees or and bushes. Well-known for the way it breaks open snail shells. Often in gardens. 23 cm.

Smaller than Mistle Thrush →

◀ Mistle Thrush

Large thrush found in most parts of Britain. Often seen on the ground in pastures and on moorland. 27 cm.

White under wing ↑

← White outer tail feathers

Starling ▶

A familiar garden bird. Often roosts in huge flocks. Mimics songs of other birds. 22 cm.

Juvenile

Adult in winter

Tits

Long-tailed Tit ▶
Hedgerows and woodland edges are good places to see groups of these tiny birds. 14 cm.

Northern and Eastern Europe

Britain and Western Europe

Black and white crest

◀ Crested Tit
Widespread in Europe but in Britain only found in a few Scottish pine woods, especially in the Spey Valley. 11 cm.

Coal Tit ▶
Likes conifer woods, but often seen in deciduous trees. Large white patch on back of head. 11 cm.

Dark line on belly

◀ Blue Tit
Seen in woods and gardens. Often raises its blue cap to form a small crest. Young are less colourful. 11 cm.

No pale patch on wings

Marsh Tit ▶
A bird of deciduous woods, like the Willow Tit (not illustrated). Rarely visits gardens. 11 cm.

Tit, Nuthatch, Treecreeper, Crests

Great Tit ▶
Largest tit. Lives in woodlands and gardens. Nests in holes in trees or will use nestboxes. 14 cm.

Broad black band on breast

◀ Nuthatch
Found in deciduous woods in England and Wales. Climbs up and down trees in a series of short hops. Very short tail. Nests in tree-holes. 14 cm.

Treecreeper ▶
Usually seen in woods climbing up tree trunks and flying down again to search for food. Listen for its high-pitched call. 13 cm.

White stripe over eye

Firecrest

◀ Firecrest
◀ Goldcrest
Smallest European birds. Goldcrests are often found in woods, especially of pine, all over Britain. Firecrests are much rarer. 9 cm.

Goldcrest

Finches

Chaffinch ▶

Likely to be found wherever there are trees and bushes, including gardens. Often flocks with other finches in winter.
15 cm.

♀

♂

Male's head is brown in winter

♂

◀ Brambling

Winter migrant from northern Europe. Flocks feed on grain and seeds. Likes fruit from beech trees.
15 cm.

♀

♂

Greenfinch ▶

A frequent visitor to gardens, especially in winter. Likely to nest wherever there are trees and bushes. 15 cm.

♀

♂

◀ Siskin

A small finch. Nests in conifers. Visits gardens in winter to feed on peanuts.
11 cm.

Finches

◀ Bullfinch

Often found on edges of woods, and in hedges or gardens. Eats seeds, but is a pest in orchards where it strips buds from fruit trees. 15 cm.

♀

♂

— White rump shows in flight

Linnet ▶

Lives on heathland and farmland, but also found in towns, where it may visit gardens. Feeds on the seeds of weeds. Flocks in winter. 13 cm.

♂

♀

Mealy Redpoll

Lesser Redpoll

◀ Lesser Redpoll
◀ Mealy Redpoll

The Lesser Redpoll is common in birch woods and forestry plantations in Britain. The Mealy lives in northern Europe. 12 cm.

Goldfinch ▶

Feeds on thistle seeds and other weed seeds in open places. Nests in trees. 12 cm.

Yellow wing bar

Crossbill, Crows

◄ Crossbill
Nests in Scottish pine woods. Rare elsewhere. Eats seeds from pine cones. 16 cm.

♀ ♂

Sparrow-sized

Jay ►
Secretive woodland bird. Will visit gardens. Listen for its harsh screeching call. Look for white rump in flight. 32 cm.

Raven ►
This large crow lives in wild rocky areas or on rocky coasts. Look for its wedge-shaped tail and huge bill. Croaks. 64 cm.

Grey on head

Jackdaw ►
Small member of the crow family. Found where there are old trees, old buildings or cliffs. Nests in colonies. Often seen with Rooks. 33 cm.

Crows

◀ **Carrion Crow**
◀ **Hooded Crow**

Carrion is seen alone or in pairs. Hooded Crows form flocks. Carrion is more widespread than Hooded . 47 cm.

Carrion Crow —
England, Wales and
southern Scotland

Hooded
Crow —
Northern
Scotland and
Ireland

Rook ▶

Nests in "rookeries" in tops of trees. Is usually seen in flocks and likes farmland. Young lack bare skin round beak. Voice is a harsh "kaw". 46 cm.

Baggy thigh feathers

◀ **Magpie**

Seen in both town and country. Eats many eggs and young birds in spring. Forms flocks in winter. 46 cm.

Sparrows, Buntings

House Sparrow ▶

Very familiar bird. Lives near houses and even in city centres, where it eats scraps, etc. Often seen in flocks.
15 cm.

♂ ♀

Brown cap and smudge below eye

Male and female look alike

◀ Tree Sparrow

Usually nests in holes in trees or cliffs. Less common than House Sparrows in towns, but sometimes flocks with them in winter. 14 cm.

Yellowhammer ▶

Common in open country, especially farmland. Feeds on the ground. Forms flocks in winter. Sings from the tops of bushes.
17 cm.

♂ ♀

♀

◀ Reed Bunting

Most common near water, but some nest in dry areas with long grass. Sometimes visits bird-tables in winter.
15 cm.

♂

Corn Bunting ▶

Quite common in cornfields. Sings from posts, bushes or overhead wires.
18 cm.

Colour the Birds

Can you identify these birds and colour them correctly? Their names are upside-down at the bottom of the page.

1 _____

2 _____

3 _____

4 _____

1. Pheasant (male) 2. Kingfisher 3. Blue Tit 4. Collared Dove

Find the Feet

Can you match the pictures of feet with the correct birds? The answers are upside-down at the bottom of the opposite page.

Cormorant —

Lesser Spotted Woodpecker —

Kingfisher —

Mallard —

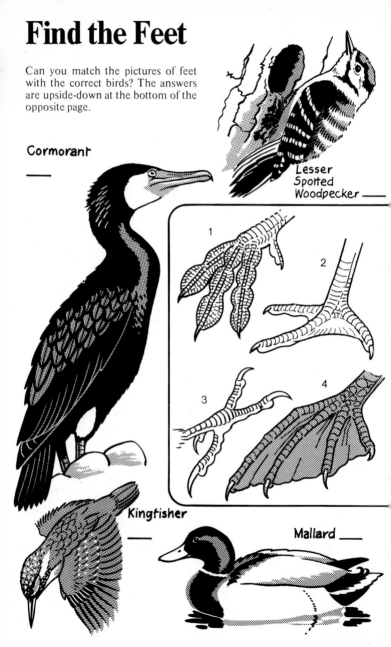

Robin ___

Golden Eagle ___

5

6

7

8

9

Tawny Owl ___

Coot ___

Oystercatcher ___

Name the Birds

Look carefully at the shapes of these birds and try to identify them. Their names are upside-down at the bottom of the opposite page.

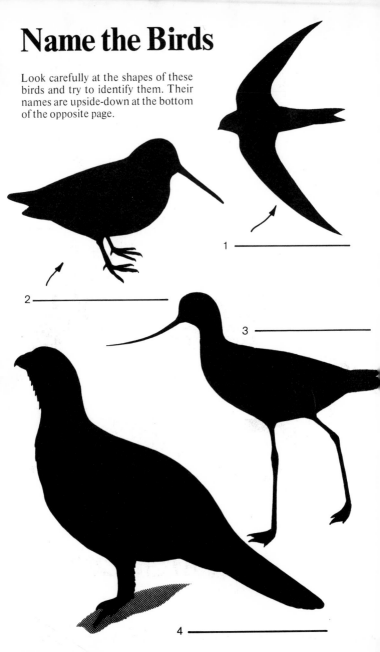

1 _____

2 _____

3 _____

4 _____

5 ————

6 ————

7 ————

8 ————

9 ————

8. Lapwing 9. Great Crested Grebe

1. Swift 2. Woodcock 3. Avocet 4. Capercaillie 5. Swallow 6. Gannet 7. Black Grouse (male

53

Making a Bird Table

Why not make a bird table for your garden or to attach to a window-sill? This is a good way to attract birds and you will be helping them to survive the winter.

Suitable foods are peanuts (not salted), pieces of apple, cereals, bacon rinds, biscuit crumbs, raisins, sunflower seeds, cooked potato and hardened fat.

Feed garden birds between October and March. There should be enough natural food for them in the summer, and some of the foods mentioned above can be harmful to young birds born in the spring.

If you put food out every day, do not stop suddenly, especially if the weather is cold, because the birds will be relying on your food supply.

Clean the bird table regularly with hot water and remove bits of old food.

These diagrams show you how to make a simple bird table. You will need: A piece of thick plywood (40 cm square), four lengths of softwood (2 cm x 2 cm x 30 cm long), eight screws and a screwdriver, glue, wood preservative and a paint-brush, nylon string and four screw eyes. You can buy these at a hardware shop.

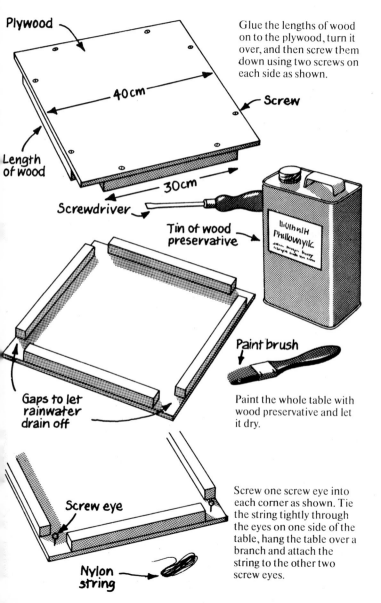

Plywood

Glue the lengths of wood on to the plywood, turn it over, and then screw them down using two screws on each side as shown.

40cm

Screw

Length of wood

30cm

Screwdriver

Tin of wood preservative

Phillowylic

Paint brush

Gaps to let rainwater drain off

Paint the whole table with wood preservative and let it dry.

Screw eye

Nylon string

Screw one screw eye into each corner as shown. Tie the string tightly through the eyes on one side of the table, hang the table over a branch and attach the string to the other two screw eyes.

Garden Bird Survey

Make a survey of the birds that visit your table, or wherever you put food out for them. You will soon learn when to expect certain birds. Try to find out which birds feed on natural foods, such as worms and berries, and which eat the scraps you put out for them. You may also be able to watch birds collecting material to build their nests. The best time to see birds is in the early morning.

The chart on this page is an example of a garden bird survey. Make a survey of the birds that visit your garden in an exercise book or in a loose leaf binder. You can make a weekly bird check instead of a monthly one if you prefer. Keep your survey up-to-date for two years to compare appearance and lengths of stay of migrating birds.

NAMES OF BIRDS SEEN	TICK OFF MONTHS YOU SEE BIRDS J F M A M J J A S O N D	FOODS EATEN		DO THEY DRINK?	DO THEY BATHE?	WHERE THEY NEST
		FOOD YOU PUT OUT	NATURAL FOOD			
HOUSE SPARROW	✓ ✓✓✓✓	BREAD		✓	✓	UNDER EAVES
ROBIN						
BLUE TIT						
GREAT TIT						
STARLING						
DUNNOCK						
BLACKBIRD						
SONG THRUSH						
GREENFINCH						
COLLARED DOVE						
PIED/WHITE WAGTAIL						
HOUSE MARTIN						
SWALLOW						
CHAFFINCH						

Glossary

Breeding season − the time of year when a pair of birds build a nest, mate, lay eggs and look after their young.

Colony - a group of birds of the same species nesting close together.

Conifers − trees, such as pines and firs, that bear cones, have needle-like leaves and are usually evergreen.

Courtship display − when a male bird attracts a mate. Some birds show off their plumage; others put on a "display" in the air.

Cover − hedges, bushes, thick grass − anywhere that birds hide themselves.

Crown − the top of a bird's head.

Juvenile − a young bird which has left the nest and whose plumage is not yet the same as its parents'.

Lek − an area where male birds gather to display to females in the breeding season.

Migration − the regular movement of birds from one place to another, from the breeding area to the area where they spend the winter. Migrating birds are called migrants or visitors.

Moult − when birds shed their old feathers and grow new ones. All birds do this at least once a year. In ducks, the duller plumage that remains after moulting is called **eclipse** plumage.

Roost − sleep. A roost is a place where birds sleep.

Rump − the lower back and base of the tail of a bird.

Species - a group of birds that all look alike and behave in the same way, e.g. the Herring Gull is the name of one species.

Books to Read

The Pocket Oxford Book of Birds. Bruce Campbell (OUP)
The RSPB Guide to British Birds. D. Saunders (Hamlyn). Two useful field guides to British birds.
A Field Guide to the Birds of Britain and Europe. R. T. Peterson, G. Mountford and P. A. D. Hollom (Collins). A very reliable field guide.
The Naturetrail Book of Birdwatching. Malcolm Hart (Usborne). Useful birdwatching tips and ideas for studying birds.
Birds. Christopher Perrins. (Collins Countryside Series). How birds live and the problems they face.
Book of British Birds. (AA/Reader's Digest). Lots of information and pictures.
The New Birdtable Book. Tony Soper (hardback David & Charles/paperback Pan). How to find out more about garden birds.
Bird Count. Humphrey Dobinson (hardback Kestrel/paperback Peacock). Practical ways to study birds.
You can buy records and tapes of bird song, or you may be able to borrow them from your library. If you want a catalogue of available records, write to the R.S.P.B., The Lodge, Sandy, Bedfordshire.

Index

Scorecard

The birds on this scorecard are arranged in the same order as they appear in the book. When you go spotting, fill in the date at the top of one of the blank columns, and then write in that column your score, next to each bird that you see. At the end of the day, add up your scores and put the total at the bottom of the columns. Then add up your grand total.

Page	Species (Name of Bird)	Score	Date	Date	Date	Page	Species (Name of Bird)	Score			
5	Shag	15				10	Goldeneye	15			
5	Gannet	20				10	Red-breasted Merganser	20			
5	Cormorant	15				10	Goosander	20			
6	Brent Goose	20				10	Shelduck	15			
6	Canada Goose	10				11	Great Crested Grebe	15			
6	Greylag Goose	15				11	Little Grebe	15			
6	Barnacle Goose	20				11	Grey Heron	10			
7	Pink-footed Goose	20				11	White Stork	25			
7	Bean Goose	25				12	Osprey	25			
7	White-fronted Goose	20				12	Golden Eagle	20			
7	Mute Swan	10				12	Red Kite	25			
7	Whooper Swan	20				13	Buzzard	15			
7	Bewick's Swan	20				13	Sparrowhawk	15			
8	Mallard	5				13	Kestrel	10			
8	Teal	15				14	Hobby	20			
8	Wigeon	15				14	Peregrine	20			
8	Pintail	20				14	Goshawk	25			
9	Shoveler	15				14	Honey Buzzard	25			
9	Pochard	15				15	Moorhen	5			
9	Tufted Duck	10				15	Coot	10			
9	Eider	15				15	Corncrake	20			
	Total						Total				

Page	Species (Name of Bird)	Score				Page	Species (Name of Bird)	Score			
15	Water Rail	15				22	Ruff	20			
16	Red Grouse	15				23	Avocet	25			
16	Willow Grouse	25				23	Woodcock	15			
16	Ptarmigan	20				23	Snipe	15			
16	Black Grouse	15				24	Woodpigeon	5			
17	Capercaillie	20				24	Stock Dove	15			
17	Partridge	10				24	Rock Dove	25			
17	Pheasant	5				24	Collared Dove	10			
17	Red-legged Partridge	15				24	Turtle Dove	15			
18	Oystercatcher	15				25	Razorbill	15			
18	Lapwing	10				25	Guillemot	15			
18	Turnstone	15				25	Fulmar	15			
19	Ringed Plover	15				25	Puffin	20			
19	Little Ringed Plover	20				26	Black-headed Gull	5			
19	Golden Plover	15				26	Lesser Black-backed Gull	10			
20	Redshank	10				26	Great Black-backed Gull	15			
20	Greenshank	20				26	Common Gull	15			
20	Common Sandpiper	15				27	Herring Gull	5			
20	Black-tailed Godwit	20				27	Common Tern	15			
21	Bar-tailed Godwit	20				27	Arctic Tern	15			
21	Curlew	15				27	Black Tern	20			
21	Whimbrel	20				27	Little Tern	20			
22	Dunlin	10				28	Barn Owl	15			
22	Knot	15				28	Little Owl	15			
22	Sanderling	15				28	Tawny Owl	15			
	Total						Total				

Page	Species (Name of Bird)	Score				Page	Species (Name of Bird)	Score			
28	Pygmy Owl	25				34	Yellow Wagtail	15			
29	Short-eared Owl	20				34	Blue-headed Wagtail	25			
29	Long-eared Owl	20				35	Waxwing	20			
29	Tengmalm's Owl	25				35	Dipper	15			
29	Scops Owl	25				35	Wren	5			
30	Hoopoe	25				35	Red-backed Shrike	25			
30	Nightjar	15				35	Great Grey Shrike	25			
30	Cuckoo	10				36	Sedge Warbler	15			
30	Kingfisher	15				36	Reed Warbler	15			
31	Great Spotted Woodpecker	10				36	Garden Warbler	15			
31	Black Woodpecker	25				36	Blackcap	15			
31	Green Woodpecker	15				37	Whitethroat	15			
31	Lesser Spotted Woodpecker	20				37	Willow Warbler	10			
32	Swift	10				37	Chiffchaff	10			
32	Swallow	10				37	Wood Warbler	15			
32	House Martin	10				38	Pied Flycatcher	15			
32	Sand Martin	15				38	Whinchat	15			
33	Skylark	10				38	Stonechat	15			
33	Crested Lark	25				38	Wheatear	15			
33	Meadow Pipit	10				39	Spotted Flycatcher	10			
33	Tree Pipit	15				39	Redstart	15			
33	Dunnock	5				39	Black Redstart	20			
34	Pied Wagtail	10				39	Robin	5			
34	White Wagtail	25				39	Nightingale	15			
34	Grey Wagtail	15				40	Fieldfare	10			
	Total						Total				

Page	Species (Name of Bird)	Score				Page	Species (Name of Bird)	Score			
40	Ring Ouzel	15				45	Mealy Redpoll	25			
40	Blackbird	5				45	Lesser Redpoll	15			
40	Golden Oriole	20				45	Goldfinch	10			
41	Redwing	10				46	Crossbill	15			
41	Song Thrush	5				46	Jay	10			
41	Mistle Thrush	10				46	Raven	15			
41	Starling	5				46	Jackdaw	10			
42	Long-tailed Tit	10				47	Carrion Crow	10			
42	Crested Tit	20				47	Hooded Crow	15			
42	Coal Tit	10				47	Rook	10			
42	Blue Tit	5				47	Magpie	10			
42	Marsh Tit	15				48	House Sparrow	5			
43	Great Tit	5				48	Tree Sparrow	15			
43	Nuthatch	15				48	Yellowhammer	10			
43	Treecreeper	10				48	Reed Bunting	15			
43	Goldcrest	10				48	Corn Bunting	15			
43	Firecrest	20									
44	Chaffinch	5									
44	Brambling	15									
44	Greenfinch	10									
44	Siskin	15									
45	Bullfinch	10									
45	Linnet	10									
	Total						Total				

Grand Total

RSPB

Birds, their nests and their eggs are protected by law, but they are still in danger. Collectors steal the eggs of rare birds, like Kites and Ospreys. Sea birds, particularly Razorbills and Guillemots, are killed by oil released into the sea. Birds of prey, Peregrines in particular, are taken from the wild and forced to spend the rest of their lives in captivity. Hunters still shoot and trap birds, both in Britain and in other European countries. Worst of all, birds' habitats (the places where birds live) are being destroyed – hedges are being dug up, ponds drained, and factories and oil refineries built in the places where birds feed and nest.

You can help birds in many ways. Feed birds during the winter so that more survive to nest the following spring. Build nestboxes to give birds somewhere safe to nest. Try to persuade your friends to take an interest in birds and their survival. Finally, you will be helping to conserve our bird life if you support the Royal Society for the Protection of Birds (R.S.P.B.) by joining its Young Ornithologists' Club (Y.O.C.).

The Y.O.C. is a national club for birdwatchers aged 15 and under. Members receive *Bird Life*, its magazine, which contains articles by experts and by members, as well as information about projects and competitions, and news about birds and club activities. The Y.O.C. has a network of over 500 adult leaders who arrange outings and meetings in many parts of Britain. The club also organizes residential courses during school holidays. As well as *Bird Life*, all members receive a free arm badge and a membership card to show that they belong to a conservation organization.

If you would like further information about the Y.O.C. and an enrolment form, please send a stamped addressed envelope to the Y.O.C., The Lodge, Sandy, Bedfordshire.